THE STORY
OF SCOTCH

by Enos Mills

Supplementary Chapters
by Kent Dannen

Alpine
Blue Ribbon Books

LOVELAND, COLORADO

S0-BTP-230

THE STORY OF SCOTCH

Copyright 1909, 1911, and 1916 by Enos A. Mills
Supplemental material © 1998 by Kent Dannen

Library of Congress Cataloging in Publication Data
Mills, Enos Abijah, 1870–1922.
    The story of Scotch / by Enos Mills; supplementary chapters by
Kent Dannen.
        p.   cm.
    ISBN 1-57779-006-5
    Border collie—Colorado—Longs Peak—Biography. 2. Dogs—
Colorado—Longs Peak Region—Biography. 3. Mills, Enos Abijah,
1870–1922.   I. Dannen, Kent. 1946- II. Title.
SF429.B64M55   1998
636.737'4—dc21   98-9772
                                                                        CIP

This book is available at special quantity discounts for breeders and
for club promotions, premiums, or educationa use. Write for details.

1 2 3 4 5 6 7 8 9 0
Cover photo courtesy of Rocky Mountain National Park.
Printed in the United States of America

To

Mary King Sherman

and

John King Sherman

Who knew and appreciated Scotch

Royalties derived from sales of this edition will be donated to the Pet Association of Estes Park, the American Dog Owner's Association, and breed rescue groups. These organizations support the bond between dogs and people that was pioneered by Mills and Scotch.

Probably the most famous and most often published photo of Enos Mills shows him sharing with Scotch their mutual love and understanding of the wilds.

TABLE OF CONTENTS

Photo by Kent and Donna Dannen

FOREWORD

by Kent Dannen

A March morning early in the twentieth century found Enos Mills facing death again. At 12,000 feet above sea level in the Colorado Rockies, the avalanche season was at its height. Every snow-filled gulch leading from a summit was a likely place to die.

As he later reported, night and clouds had caught Mills on a promontory high above tree line. He had to exercise constantly to keep from freezing. Dawn had been brilliant on the tops of low-lying clouds, but now he was descending through them and could see only a few feet in any direction. Moving a few inches at each step, he zigzagged down an incredibly steep slope on skis.

Finally, the pitch became less precipitous, allowing more normal skiing. As morning sun burned away the clouds, Mills could see where he was. Behind and above, his ski tracks zigzagged down 1,000 feet of the sheer walls of a rocky amphitheater. He now stood at a point where the walls of the amphitheater were lower and pinched together, forming a narrow gulch about two miles long.

Except in a small space where Mills had begun his descent, a huge snow cornice rimmed the amphitheater. He could see that when the cornice fell, hundreds of tons of snow would rush down the gulch, grinding to splinters everything in the way. Just as he was thinking that the cornice could fall any second, it did. Mills whirled and skied down the gulch, the only possible direction of escape. Thirty seconds later, the avalanche crashed over where he had stood and pursued him down the gulch.

Jumping over ridges and across gullies, he raced down the narrow, rocky defile as the slide gained on him. With only a ten-foot staff instead of ski poles, Mills wove a desperate slalom through the close-growing fir trees at tree line.

A slight widening in the track ahead indicated that a side canyon might offer a haven out of the slide's path. Then his coat snagged on a tree branch. Thrown off balance, Mills smashed his left ski against another tree. Only his staff kept him from falling.

He could not race far with a broken ski. So close was the avalanche behind him that he could hear boulders and broken trees grinding within its mass. Mills desperately threw away his staff and flung himself down the slope with uncontrolled speed. An awkward turn dumped him head-over-heels into the side canyon and safety.

The event was not unique in Mills' life. His experiences in the Rockies with snowslides, cliffs, lightning, forest fires, and wild animals would have made good episodes for serialized motion pictures. In this book, Mills tells about some of these adventures that involved his dog Scotch.

Mills calls Scotch a "collie." Photos indicate that Scotch was a Border Collie, rather than the breed made famous in subsequent decades by Lassie. Sheepherders in the Scottish Highlands still sometimes refer to Border Collies as "collie dogs."

Virtually all of his adventure stories reflect poorly on Mills' good sense as a mountaineer. However, his frequent risk-taking derived from his fervent belief that wild lands actually were safety zones amid the dangerous complexities of modern civilization. Perhaps his accounts of near disasters resulting from his own mistakes were an effective argument for his creed of friendly and safe wilderness: If someone as reckless as Mills survived, how dangerous could the wilds be?

Despite his lack of prudence (or perhaps in part because of it), Mills inspired thousands to join him in his love for wilderness. A large audience enjoyed his many articles and sixteen books about the wild and scenic in America. Also, he was a popular lecturer all over the country. His work climaxed in 1915 when Congress established Rocky Mountain National Park in the Longs Peak region of Colorado.

Mills modeled his work after that of John Muir, then as now America's best-known prophet of wilderness preservation. They met on a beach in San Francisco in 1889, when fires in a Montana copper mine left Mills temporarily unemployed and free to travel. A chance conversation between two strangers, each interested intensely in nature, was a turning point in Mills' life. Mills was nineteen; Muir was fifty-one. Despite their age difference, they became friends.

Both Muir and Mills loved to roam in wild mountains. Since leaving his parents' eastern Kansas farm for Colorado at age fourteen, Mills had spent his summers wandering around his cabin near Longs Peak. When winter came, he worked on ranches or in mines to support his summer rambles.

Muir gave direction to Mills' life and encouraged his desire to learn about the way nature worked. Furthermore, John Muir inspired Enos Mills to join the crusade to save the wilderness in order that others could experience its joys and learn from it.

With encouragement from Muir, Mills began in 1890 to write articles about his wilderness experiences for newspapers and magazines. In 1905, he was his own publisher for his first book, *The Story of Estes Park and a Guide Book.* It sold well, and his books did not again lack a commercial publisher in his lifetime. *The Story of Scotch* is the ninth brought back into print for modern wilderness enthusiasts.

Among the most popular of Mills' writings were stories about his winter adventures in the high mountains. Many of these adventures occurred when he gave up mining and, during the winters of 1902 through 1905, worked as a Colorado Snow Observer. (He also acquired Scotch in 1902.) On perilous patrols along the crests of Colorado mountain ranges, he measured the snow accumulation in order that the Colorado Department of Irrigation could predict the amount of spring runoff. His courage and temperament were uniquely suited to this dangerous and solitary job.

On one winter trip, what Mills had taken for a settler's cabin turned out to be a mountain schoolhouse, complete with a new school marm from the East and six pupils. Mills at that time was two days past his last food and looked rather disheveled with his face blackened by charcoal for protection against sunburn. Despite second thoughts about desperadoes of popular western fiction, the teacher let the Colorado Snow Observer in, and the children gave him parts of their lunches. He then delivered to his benefactors an after-dinner speech on forestry and conservation.

Mills conducted his own nature school after buying Longs Peak Inn, also in the eventful year of 1902. The main form of recreation for children and adults was hiking on trails that led up and around Longs Peak. A "nature guide," often Mills himself, frequently accompanied these hikers.

Jack London's novel *Call of the Wild* contrasted traits of civilization and wilderness as evident in a dog and gained wide popularity in 1903. Mills' adopted "Call of the Wild" as a catch phrase to symbolize the emphasis of his nature-guide program at Longs Peak Inn. His nature guides pioneered modern nature interpretation programs of the National Park Service and many other government and private agencies that manage natural lands.

Many of the inn's (often illustrious and politically active) guests considered Scotch to be Mills' co-host at the establishment. For instance, Mary King Sherman, to whom Mills dedicated *The Story of Scotch*, was a national park advocate and prominent president of the General Federation of Women's Clubs. She also was a frequent guest at Longs Peak Inn and one of Mills' main allies in the fight for Rocky Mountain National Park.

On the national park's highest mountain, Longs Peak, Mills delegated to Scotch the role of guide for an admirable but inexperienced climber. In the less wild setting of the inn itself, Scotch performed antics such as playing "football" with a round ball. Mills probably was using football as the English do to describe the game that Americans call soccer.

The significant entertainment value that Scotch had for Longs Peak Inn guests and staff may be difficult for some people in this television-dominated age to understand. Yet, even today in a somewhat analogous setting in Alaska's Denali National Park, the sled dog demonstrations run by the National Park Service are among the park's most popular programs.

An all-consuming fire destroyed Longs Peak Inn at the beginning of the tourist season in 1906. Undiscouraged, Mills used the disaster as an opportunity to further manifest the "Call of the Wild" by using his naturalist's imagination when choosing materials to rebuild. In order to avoid cutting living trees and because standing-dead trunks were less likely to shrink or warp, Mills used fire-killed logs for the main structure of the rebuilt inn. Beaver-gnawed logs and roots of dead trees accented the interior. Individual wildflowers on tables occasionaly provided bits of color to this wild architecture, though Mills preached against picking large bouquets.

To preserve the wild charms of the Colorado Rockies had become Mills' goal after meeting John Muir. In 1909, he began working toward this goal by devoting his full energy to creation of Rocky Mountain National Park around Longs Peak Inn.

At first, many of his neighbors in Colorado were indifferent to the idea. Mills turned to the East for support that he lacked at home. The Colorado innkeeper lectured to many receptive audiences about the beauties of the Rockies and how unwise, selfish exploitation threatened these beauties. The press was sympathetic to his cause, and editors were eager to get firsthand information about national park issues. Their support resulted in much publicity for Mills' park plan.

The popularity of the proposal in the East enthused people at home. Soon, however, local opposition developed and hostility toward formation of Rocky Mountain National Park spread among Mills' neighbors and former friends.

Mills believed that the United States Department of Agriculture's Forest Service was a moving force behind opposition to creation of the park. The Forest Service was in charge of most of the proposed park's lands. Mills believed that the Forest Service would lose political power derived from granting lumbering and grazing permits if Congress banned these activities in a national park or if park land administration moved to the Department of the Interior. Therefore, Mills reasoned that the Forest Service was eager to prevent park formation by hook or by crook.

The Forest Service denied Mills' accusations and claimed to favor establishment of Rocky Mountain National Park. Forest Service letters and statements about the issue indicated a somewhat ambivalent bureaucracy, struggling with itself, with other government agencies, and with Mills to refine its own role in federal land management in the West. As controversy boiled in this refining fire, many people suffered burns to their egos, leading to broken friendships and bitterness.

Bitterness was not, fortunately, universal or irreversible. One winter night, when the temperature was as cold as the controversy was hot, one of the park's most active opponents turned up on Mills' doorstep in desperate need of help. Caught by the cold, the opponent had badly frostbitten feet and was exhausted by his struggle against the elements. Mills later recounted his treating the man's feet well enough to save them and then converting him to the park cause.

To appease economic interests that feared being locked out of natural resource use by a national park, Mills compromised by agreeing to various reductions in size of his original park proposal. On Muir's advice, Mills traveled widely over America to win more allies, delivering forty-two speeches in favor of the park. He encouraged regional mountaineering clubs and other organizations, including the Colorado Mountain Club, to support national parks. He lobbied in Washington, D.C. He wrote more than two thousand letters and sixty-four articles for newspapers and magazines to promote creating the park. His personal funds evaporated in the six years of effort. Finally, in January 1915, Congress passed the bill creating Rocky Mountain National Park. Everywhere Mills was called its father.

The park's dedication the following September was Mills' best public hour. Yet, photos of him at the event do not show the joy that, for instance, we see in photos of him playing with Scotch. As everyone else celebrated the birth of the national park, Mills appeared to have other things on his mind. Among these other concerns were areas dropped from his original park proposal. Congress added some of these areas to the park in a 1917 victory.

Throughout the rest of his life, Mills was ever ready to defend the park he had labored so hard to create. However, while visiting New York City in 1922, he suffered an injury in a subway accident. A few weeks later, the mountaineer who had demonstrated that the wilderness was a safety zone ironically proved his point by dying of complications from injuries received in the city. The direct cause was dental surgery, which in that era sometimes was fatal to patients in rundown condition.

Besides his theme of the wilderness as a safety zone, Mills maintained that play was a common activity among animals. Mills believed that the play or fun part of animals' lives was very significant in how animals contributed to wilderness values. Furthermore, he viewed the play of wild animals as being essentially similar to that of domestic animals or of humans. Play was a mystic continuum benefitting butterflies, beavers, and bears as well as dogs and people.

Play as an element in animals' lives was a topic of scientific discussion in Mills' day as it is in ours. Few scientists today would extend the notion of play to butterflies, which doubtless would irritate Mills, who shared with John Muir a lack of sympathy for coldly objective science. Among mammals, however, modern science generally accepts the importance of play.

For all he talked about play being important, Mills did not engage in much himself. Throughout his life, much of his work was what most people did for play during vacations. Yet the endless details of being an innkeeper and a park advocate were not play by anyone's definition. Colorado tradition holds that Mills literally worked and worried himself into an early grave during controversy about national park management. A less intense worker would have recovered completely from his New York injuries to face dental surgery unimpaired.

The importance of play in Mills' understanding of the wilderness and its creatures adds significance to his wilderness experiences with Scotch. For instance, Mills described Scotch as being capable of make-believe play and, in other books, attributed the same capacity to wild animals. His experiences with Scotch made it easier for Mills to perceive a play relationship among wild, domestic, and human animals. Mills' concept of play as an essential wilderness value makes *The Story of Scotch* important to the complete understanding of Mills' longer books.

His longer books, however, reveal the importance of play in wilderness values more completely than does *The Story of Scotch*. Without some knowledge of Mills' play concept from his other books, it is easy to overlook the significance of statements like "Scotch enjoyed being with me, and great times we had together," or "Through the seasons and through the years Scotch and I wandered in the wilds and enjoyed nature together," or "Scotch was not there to cheer the wintry, silent scene," or the descriptions of Scotch at play around Longs Peak Inn.

Scotch may have helped Mills develop his notion of play, one of his most important observations about wilderness. Furthermore, his eight years roaming the Rocky Mountain wilderness in company with Scotch gave Mills the core experiences for his later writings and inspired his crusades. They were also his happiest years, excluding perhaps the few years at the end of his life. In his last years, however, the great joys of marriage and fatherhood stood in stark contrast to his great frustrations over what he understood to be betrayal of national park principles by former allies.

It is more than coincidence that Mills' most productive years for understanding wilderness values were those years that he spent with Scotch. Not only did Scotch teach Mills about wild animals by providing a valid and easy-to-understand analogy to them, but Scotch also helped Mills himself experience the importance of play in his own life.

Whether by coincidence or through lack of canine stimulus, Mills' own play seems to have diminished after Scotch's accidental death in 1910. Some neighbors and relatives, who became estranged from Mills during national park controversies, claimed that his personality changed. Speaking as his enemies, they attributed the change to his becoming arrogant due to national acclaim. (For instance, 1910 was the first year Mills appeared in *Who's Who*.)

Even the biased observations of enemies might have contained a hint of truth. Seriousness, always present in Mills' personality, lost a balancing influence that a dog might have provided, at least until marriage brightened Mills' personal life in 1919. Controversies over public land management as well as increasing business pressures by 1919 might have worn seriousness as a deep rut in the crusader's personality. Given time, his wife (who was a remarkably appropriate match for Mills) and his daughter probably would have smoothed such a rut. Unfortunately, they did not have much time.

The various aspects of Mills' seriousness—stress, overwork, ill-will growing from controversy over national park management—allowed a city injury to weaken a wilderness prophet. He often had neglected to follow what he knew to be safe practices in mountaineering and managed to get away with it. When he failed to copy at least temporarily the carefree attitudes he had seen of wolves chasing tumbleweeds or a grizzly cub playing with Scotch, Mills became vulnerable to the circumstances that killed him.

Recent scientific discovery of the great importance of pets to human health provides a strong base for believing that the loss of Scotch and the failure to replace him indirectly caused Mills' premature death at age fifty-three. This realization makes all the more gut-wrenching the already stark last words of *The Story of Scotch* ("He was instantly killed").

The explosion fatal to Scotch probably occurred during the blasting of comparatively shallow road cuts for Colorado Highway 7 in front of Longs Peak Inn. Thus, Scotch became the first dog in this region killed by modern automotive transportation.

Why Mills did not get another dog is completely speculative. Scotch was a gift, which perhaps no one sought to repeat. Given Scotch's popularity and the nationwide notice of his death, however, it seems likely that Mills received offers of new dogs. In the midst of a very time-consuming crusade for the national park, Mills may have preferred to put off acquiring a puppy, which would have consumed much more time than an adult dog.

In some people, especially those of sensitive or serious temperament, the death of a much-treasured dog kills also the desire for another pet. Such a response may be more likely if the dog's death is sudden and premature. Popular British poet Rudyard Kipling expressed this response with the advice, "Brothers and Sisters, I bid you beware / Of giving your heart to a dog to tear." The poem appeared in a 1909 anthology. Mills may or may not have read it, although as widely read as Mills was, he certainly knew some of Kipling's work. If not the poem itself, then its sentiment as well as the work of establishing the national park may have prevented Mills from acquiring a new dog.

The emotion which Kipling reflects can be deadly if it deprives a person of the daily emotion-lifting diversion that a pet can provide. Mills was right about the critical importance of play and diversion to animal well-being, whether that of a grizzly bear, a Border Collie, or a father of a national park.

Scotch helped Mills realize the importance of play to wild animals and to people in wild or domestic settings. This perhaps is the main reason *The Story of Scotch* is valuable to modern readers, whether they are interested in dogs or interested in wilderness, and especially if they are, like Mills, interested in both.

Kent Dannen
Tahosa Valley, 1997

Samoyed and owner enjoy sunrise by the lake.

PREFACE

by Enos Mills

SCOTCH and I were companions through eight years. Winter and summer we explored the rugged mountains of the Continental Divide. Often we were cold; more often we were hungry. Together we fought our way through blizzards and forest fires. Never did he complain and at all times he showed remarkable intelligence and absolute fidelity. The thousands who have watched him play football by my cabin on the slope of Long's Peak and the other thousands who have read of his unusual experiences will be interested, I am sure, in this complete story of his life.

I gave an account of Scotch in my *Wild Life on the Rockies,* and in *The Spell of the Rockies* I related one of our winter experiences. These chapters and an article on him which I wrote for *Country Life in America* are, together with additional matter, embodied in this little book.

THE STORY OF SCOTCH

I

A famous collie and her five little puppies came into the possession of a Swedish farmer of my acquaintance. For an unimportant and forgotten kindness which I had shown his children, he decided that I should have one of these promising puppies. To his delight I chose the "wisest one," wee "Scotch," who afterwards gave pleasure to hundreds of people and who for eight years was a factor in my life.

I carried little Scotch all day long in my overcoat pocket as I rode through the mountains on the way to my cabin. His cheerful

*This Border Collie is similar in appearance to the puppy
Scotch that grew to be Mills' important aide in understanding
and interpreting Rocky Mountain wilderness.*
PHOTO BY KENT AND DONNA DANNEN

little face, his good behavior, and the bright way in which he poked his head out of my pocket, licked my hand, and looked at the scenery completely won my heart before I had ridden an hour.

We camped for the night by a dim road near a deserted ranch-house in the mountains. Scotch was quiet during the long ride, but while I was lighting the camp-fire he climbed out of my overcoat and proceeded, puppy fashion, to explore the camp. After one bark at my pony he went over to make her acquaintance. He playfully smelled each of her feet, gave a happy bark, and jumped up to touch her nose with his own. Cricket, the pony, intently watched his performance with lowered head and finally nosed him in a friendly manner.

*Mills rests from wilderness exploration with his horse Cricket
and his dog Scotch. Mills saw wild and domestic animals
as fundamentally united with people as merely
variations in the stream of life rather than
as distinct kinds of beings.*
DENVER PUBLIC LIBRARY, WESTERN HISTORY DEPARTMENT

I shut him up in a small abandoned cabin for the night. He at once objected and set up a terrible barking and howling, gnawing fiercely at the crack beneath the door and trying to tear his way out. Fearing he would break his little puppy teeth, or possibly die from frantic and persistent efforts to be free, I concluded to release him from the cabin. My fears that he would run away if left free were groundless. He made his way to my saddle, which lay on the ground near by, crawled under it, turned round beneath it, thrust his little head from beneath the arch of the horn, and lay down with a look of contentment, and also with an air which said: "I'll take care of this saddle. I'd like to see any one touch it."

And watch it he did. At midnight a cow-boy came to my camp-fire. He had been thrown from his bronco and was making back to his outfit on foot. Tiny Scotch flew at him ferociously; never have I seen such faithful ferocity in a dog so small and young. I took him in my hands and assured him that the visitor was welcome, and in a moment little Scotch and the cowboy were side by side gazing at the fire.

On our arrival at my cabin he at once took possession of an old tub in a corner of the porch. This he liked, and it remained his kennel for a long time. Here, protected from wind and rain, he was comfortable even in cold weather.

We were intimate from the start, and we lived most of the time apart from the world.

I watched his development with satisfaction. He grew rapidly in size, strength, comprehension, and accomplishments. He was watchful and fearless through life.

His first experience with the unfriendly side of life came from a burro. A prospector came by with one of these long-eared beasts. Confiding Scotch went out to play with the burro and was kicked. Thenceforward he looked upon all burros with distrust, and every one that came near the cabin promptly and precipitously retreated before him like a boy before an aggressive bumblebee.

The summer that Scotch was growing up, I raised Johnny, a jolly young grizzly bear. At first the smaller, Johnny early became the larger. Both these youngsters were keenly alert, playful, and inclined to be friendly.

Each, however, was a trifle suspicious of the other. Unfortunately, I was away during the period in which a complete understanding between them could have been established and, as a result, there never came about the intimate companionship that really should have existed between these two highly developed animals; but their relations, though ever peculiar, were never strained. At times both had the freedom of the yard at once, and naturally they sometimes met while going to and fro. On these occasions each passed the other by as though unconscious of his presence.

Sometimes they lay at close range for an hour at a time, quietly, half-admiringly watching each other. A bone was used as a medium the few times they played together. Each in turn guarded this bone while the other tried to take it away. This brought out from both a lively lot of striking, feinting, boxing, dodging, and grabbing, which usually ended in clinching and wrestling. In these vigorous, though good-natured mix-ups, it was Johnny's idea to get in a few good bites on Scotch's shaggy tail; while on the end of Johnny's sensitive nose Scotch landed slap after slap.

Scotch was an old-fashioned collie and had a face that was exceptionally expressive and pleasing. He was short-nosed, and his fine eyes were set wide apart. When grown he was a trifle larger than the average dog, and was surprisingly agile and powerful for his size. His coat was a shaggy silky black, with feet, tip of tail, and breast of pure white. He was always well dressed and took good care of his coat and feet. Daily he immersed himself in the cold waters of the brook, when it was not frozen, and he frequently lay in the water, lapping it and enjoying himself.

I never knew of his killing anything, though often in the woods he merrily chased the lively, playful chipmunks. Never, however, did he disturb bird or chipmunk in the yard around the cabin. Often two or three chipmunks romped over him as he lay, with half-shut eyes, near the door. Occasionally a bird hopped upon him, and frequently birds, chipmunks, and Scotch ate together from the same bowl.

Scotch did but little barking. In the country most dogs bow-wow at strangers, and frequently make the night hideous with prolonged barking at far-off sounds or imaginary objects. In summer Scotch allowed the scores of daily callers to come and go without a bark, but he reserved the right to announce, with a bark or two, the approach of the semi-occasional stranger who invaded our winter isolation.

Talking to animals appears to make them gentler and more responsive. Scotch never tired of listening to me, and I often talked to him as if he were a child. He came to understand many of the words used. If I said "hatchet," he hastened to bring it; if "fire," he at once endeavored to discover where it was. Cheerfully and intelligently he endeavored to help me, and early became efficient in driving cattle, horses, and burros. Instinctively he was a "heeler," and with swift heel nips quickly awakened and gave directions to lazy or unwilling "critters."

II

Many of Scotch's actions were beyond the scope of instinct. One day, when still young, he mastered a new situation by the use of his wits. While he was alone at the house, some frightened cattle smashed a fence about a quarter of a mile away and broke into the pasture. He was after them in an instant. From a mountain-side ledge above, I watched proceedings with a glass. The cattle were evidently excited by the smell of some animal and did not drive well. Scotch ignored the two pasture gates, which were closed, and endeavored to hurry the cattle out through the break through which they had entered. After energetic encouragement, all but one went flying out through the break. This one alternated between stupidly running back and forth along the fence and trying to gore Scotch. Twice the animal had run into a corner by one of the gates, and his starting for the corner the third time apparently gave Scotch an idea. He stopped heeling, raced for the gate, and, leaping up, bit at the handle of the sliding wooden bar that secured it. He repeated this biting and tearing at the handle until the bar slid and the gate swung open. After chasing the animal through, he lay down by the gate.

When I came into view he attracted my attention with sharp barks and showed great

Mills and Scotch wait at the gate to Longs Peak Inn to welcome visitors to Tahosa Valley. Lily Mountain rises in the background.
ROCKY MOUNTAIN NATIONAL PARK PHOTO

delight when I closed the gate. After this, he led me to the break in the fence and then lay down. Though I looked at him and asked, "What do you want done here?" he pretended not to hear. That was none of his business!

He had much more individuality than most dogs. His reserve force and initiative usually enabled him to find a way and succeed with situations which could not be mastered in his old way. The gate-opening was one of the many incidents in which these traits brought triumph.

One of his most remarkable achievements was the mastering of a number of cunning coyotes which were persistent in annoying him and willing to make an opportunity to kill him. In a sunny place close to the cabin, the coyotes one autumn frequently collected for a howling concert. This irritated Scotch, and he generally chased the howlers into the woods. Now and then he lay down on their yelping-grounds to prevent their prompt return. After a time these wily little wolves adopted tantalizing tactics, and one day, while Scotch was chasing the pack, a lame coyote made a detour and came behind him. In the shelter of a willow-clump the coyote broke out in a maddening Babel of yelps and howls. Scotch instantly turned back to suppress him. While he was thus busy, the entire pack doubled back into the open and taunted Scotch with attitude and howls.

Twice did the pack repeat these annoying, defying tactics. This serious situation put Scotch on his mettle. One night he went down the mountain to a ranch-house fifteen miles away. For the first time he was gone all night. The next morning I was astonished to find another collie in Scotch's bed. Scotch was in a state of worried suspense until I welcomed the stranger; then he was most gleeful. This move on his part told plainly that he was planning something still more startling. Indeed he was, but never did I suspect what this move was to be.

That day, at the first howl of the coyotes, I rushed out to see if the visiting collie would assist Scotch. There were the coyotes in groups of two and three, yelping, howling, and watching. Both dogs were missing, but presently they came into view, cautiously approaching the coyotes from behind a screen of bushes. Suddenly the visiting collie dashed out upon them. At the same instant Scotch leaped into a willow-clump and crouched down; it was by this clump that the lame coyote had each time come to howl behind Scotch.

While the visiting collie was driving the pack, the lame coyote again came out to make his sneaking flank movement. As he rounded the willow-clump Scotch leaped upon him. Instantly the other dog raced back, and both dogs fell fiercely upon the coyote. Though lame, he was powerful, and finally shook the dogs off and escaped to the woods, but he was badly wounded and bleeding freely. The pack fled and came no more to howl near the cabin.

At bedtime, when I went out to see the dogs, both were away. Their tracks in the road showed that Scotch had accompanied the neighboring collie at least part of the way home.

On rare occasions Scotch was allowed to go with visitors into the woods or up the mountain-side. However, he was allowed to accompany only those who appreciated the companionship and the intelligence of a noble dog or who might need him to show the way home.

One day a young woman from Michigan came along and wanted to climb Long's Peak alone and without a guide. I agreed to consent to her wish if she would take Scotch with her and would also first climb one of the lesser peaks on a stormy day, unaided. This climbing the young woman did, and by so doing convinced me that she had a keen sense of direction and an abundance of strength, for the day was a stormy one and the peak was completely befogged with clouds. After this there was nothing for me to do but to allow her to climb Long's Peak.

Just as she was starting for Long's Peak that cool September morning, I called Scotch and said to him: "Scotch, go with this young woman up Long's Peak. Keep her on the trail, take good care of her, and stay with her until she returns!" Scotch gave a few barks of satisfaction and started with the young woman up the trail, carrying himself in a manner which indicated that he was both honored and pleased. I felt that the strength and alertness of the young woman, when combined with the faithfulness and watchfulness of Scotch, would make the ascent a success, for the dog knew the trail as well as any guide.

The young woman climbed swiftly until she reached the rocky alpine moorlands above timber-line. Here she lingered long to enjoy the magnificent scenery and the brilliant flowers. It was late in the afternoon when she arrived at the summit of the Peak. After she had spent a little time there, resting and absorbing the beauty and grandeur of the scene, she started to return. She had not gone far when clouds and darkness came on, and on a slope of slide rock she turned aside from the trail.

Scotch had minded his own affairs and enjoyed himself in his own way all day long. Most of the time he had followed her closely, apparently indifferent to what happened. But the instant the young woman left the trail and started off in the wrong direction, he sprang ahead and took the lead with an alert, aggressive air. The way in which he did this should have suggested to her that he knew what he was about, but she did not appreciate this fact. She thought he had become weary and wanted to run away from her, so she called him back. Again she started in the wrong direction. This time Scotch got in front of her and refused to move. She pushed him out of the way. Once more he started off in the right direction and this time she scolded him and reminded him that his master had told him to stay with her. Scotch dropped his ears, fell in behind her, and followed meekly in her steps. He had tried to carry out the first part of his master's orders;

now he was resigned to the second part of them.

After going a short distance, the young woman realized that she had lost her trail but it never occurred to her that she had only to let Scotch have his way and he would lead her safely home. However, she had the good sense to stop where she was. And there, among the crags, by the stained remnants of winter's snow, thirteen thousand feet above sea-level, she knew she must pass the night. The wind blew a gale and the alpine brooklet turned to ice, while, in the lee of a crag, shivering with cold and hugging Scotch tight, she lay down to wait for daylight.

When darkness had come that evening and the young woman had not returned, I sent a rescue party of four guides up the

Peak. They suffered much from cold as they vainly searched among the crags through the dark hours of the windy night. Just at sunrise one of the guides found her. She was almost exhausted, but was still hugging Scotch tightly and only her fingers were frostbitten. The guide gave her wraps and food and drink, and started with her down the trail. And Scotch? Oh, as soon as the guide appeared he left her and started home for breakfast. Scotch saved this young woman's life by staying with her through the long, cold night. She appreciated the fact, and was quick to admit that if she had allowed the dog to have his own way about the trail she would have had no trouble.

III

One summer a family lived in a cabin at the farther side of the big yard. Scotch developed a marked fondness for the lady of the house and called on her daily. He was so purposeful about this that from the moment he rose to start there was no mistaking his plans. Along the pathway toward the cabin he went, evidently with something definite in his mind. He was going somewhere; there was no stopping, no hurrying, and no turning aside. If the door was open, in he went; if it was closed, he made a scraping stroke across it and with dignified pose waited for it to be opened. Inside he was the gentleman. Generally he made a quiet tour through all the rooms and then lay down before the fireplace. If any one talked to him, he watched the speaker and listened with pleased attention; if the speaker was animated, Scotch now and then gave a low bark of appreciation. Usually he stayed about half an hour and then went sedately out. Without looking back, he returned deliberately to his own quarters.

What an unconscious dignity there was in his make-up! He would not "jump for the gentleman," nor leap over a stick, nor "roll over." No one ever would have thought of asking him to speak, to say grace, or to sit up on his hind legs for something to eat. All these tricks were foreign to his nature and had no place in his philosophy!

Though Scotch admitted very few to the circle of his intimate friends, he was admired, respected, and loved by thousands. One of these admirers writes of him: "Of this little rustic Inn, Scotch was no less the host than was his master. He welcomed the coming and sped the parting guest. He escorted the climbers to the beginning of the trail up Long's Peak. He received the returning trout fishermen. He kept the burros on the other side of the brook. He stood between the coyotes and the inhabitants of the chicken yard. He was always ready to play football for the entertainment of the guests after dinner. He was really the busiest person about the Inn from morning till night."

Though apparently matter-of-fact and stolid, he was ever ready for a romp and was one of the most playful dogs. Except at odd times, I was the only playmate he ever had. It was a pleasure to watch him or to play with him, for he played with all his might. He took an intense delight in having me kick or toss a football for him. He raced at full speed in pursuing the ball, and upon overtaking it would try to pick it up, but it was too large for him. As soon as I picked it up, he became all alert to race after it or to leap up and intercept it. If the ball was tossed easily to him, he sprang to meet it and usually struck it with the point of his chin and sent it flying back to me; at short range we were sometimes able to send the ball back and forth between us several times without either one

The Story of Scotch

*A Border Collie similar in appearance to Scotch plays
with a tennis ball. Scotch played with a much larger ball to
the delight of Longs Peak Inn guests.
Scotch's play with a ball and in many other situations
helped Mills learn about the importance of play
in the lives of wild animals.*

PHOTO BY KENT AND DONNA DANNEN

moving in his tracks. If the ball was tossed above him, he leaped up to strike it with head, chin, or teeth, trying to make it bound upward; if it went up, he raced to do it over again. Occasionally he was clever enough to repeat this many times without allowing the ball to fall to the earth.

His enjoyment in make-believe play was as eager and refreshing as that of a child. This kind of play we often enjoyed in the yard. I would pretend to be searching for him, while he, crouching near in plain view, pretended to be hidden. Oh, how he enjoyed this! Again and again I would approach him from a different direction, and, when within touching distance, call, "Where is Scotch?" while he, too happy for barks, hugged the earth closely and silently. Now and then he took a pose and pretended to be looking at something far away, while all the time his eager eye was upon me. From time to time, with utmost stealth, he took a new hiding place. With every pretense of trying not to be seen, he sometimes moved from behind to immediately in front of me! Silently, though excitedly happy, he played this delightful childish game. It always ended to his liking; I grabbed him with a "Hello, there's Scotch!" and carried him off on my shoulder.

One day a family arrived at a nearby cottage to spend the summer. During the first afternoon of their stay, the toddling baby strayed away. Every one turned out to search. With enlarging circles we covered the surrounding country and at last came upon the youngster in the woods about a quarter of a mile from the house. Scotch was with him and was lying down with head up, while the baby, asleep, was using him for a pillow, and had one chubby arm thrown across his neck. He saw us approach and left the baby as if nothing unusual had happened.

He never failed to notice my preparations to journey beyond the mountains. Never would he watch me start on this kind of a journey, but an hour or so before leaving-time he would go to the side of the house opposite where I started. Here he would refuse attention from any one and for a few days would go about sadly.

A little in advance of my homecoming, he showed that he expected me. Probably he heard my name used by the people in the house. Anyway, for two or three days before my arrival, he each evening would go down the road and wait at the place where he had greeted me many times on my return.

When I went horseback-riding he was almost passionately happy if allowed to go along. Whenever my pony was brought out, he at once stopped everything and lay down near the pony to await my coming. Would I go out on the trail with him, or go to the post office and leave him behind? By the time I appeared, these questions had him in a high state of excitement. Usually he turned his head away and yawned and yawned; he rose up and sat down, altogether showing a strange combination of bashfulness and impatience; though plainly trying to be quiet, he was restless until my answer came. Usually he was able to make out what this was without waiting for any word from me. A hatchet, for example, would tell him I was going to the woods. On the other hand, the mailbag meant that I was going to the village. This meant that he could not go, whereupon he would go off slowly, lie down, and look the other way.

If the answer was "yes," he raced this way and that, leaping up once or twice to touch the pony's nose with his own. During each ride he insisted on a race with the pony; if I chanced to forget this, he never failed to remind me before the ride was over. As a reminder, he would run alongside me and leap as high as possible, then race ahead as swiftly as he could. This he repeated until I accepted his challenge. Both dog and pony gleefully enjoyed this and each tried to pass the other.

Once we were clattering over the last stretch toward home. Scotch, who was in the lead, saw our pet chicken crouched in the pony's track, where it was in danger of being crushed. Unmindful of his own danger from the pony's hoofs, he swerved, gently caught up the chicken, and lifted it out of danger. After fondling it for a moment, he raced after us at full speed.

No matter what the weather, he usually slept outdoors. He understood, however, that he was welcome to come into my cabin day or night, and was a frequent caller. In the cabin he was dignified and never used it as a place of amusement.

IV

Scotch enjoyed being with me, and great times we had together. Many of our best days were in the wilds. Here he often suffered from hunger, cold, hardships, and sometimes from accident; yet never did he complain. Usually he endured the unpleasant things as a matter of course.

Though very lonely when left by himself, he never allowed this feeling to cause a slighting of duty. On one occasion he was supremely tried but did his duty as he understood it and was faithful under circumstances of loneliness, danger, and possible death.

At the close of one of our winter trips, Scotch and I started across the Continental Divide of the Rocky Mountains in face of weather conditions that indicated a snow-storm or a blizzard before we could gain the other side. We had eaten the last of our food twenty-four hours before, and could no longer wait for fair weather. So off we started to scale the snowy steeps of the cold, gray heights a thousand feet above. The mountains already were deeply snow-covered and it would have been a hard trip even without the discomforts and dangers of a storm.

I was on snowshoes, and for a week we had been camping and tramping through the snowy forests and glacier meadows at the source of Grand River, two miles above the sea. The primeval Rocky Mountain forests are just as near to Nature's heart in winter as in summer. I had found so much to study and enjoy that the long distance from a food-supply, even when the last mouthful was eaten, had not aroused me to the seriousness of the situation. Scotch had not complained, and appeared to have the keenest collie interest in the tracks and trails, the scenes and silences away from the haunts of man. The snow lay seven feet deep, but by keeping in my snow-shoe-tracks Scotch easily followed me about. Our last camp was in the depths of an alpine forest, at an altitude of ten thousand feet. Here, though zero weather prevailed, we were easily comfortable beside a fire under the protection of an overhanging cliff.

After a walk through the woods the sun came blazing in our faces past the snow-piled crags on Long's Peak, and threw slender blue shadows of the spiry spruces far out in a white glacier meadow to meet us. Re-entering the tall but open woods, we saw, down the long aisles and limb-arched avenues, a forest of tree columns, entangled in sunlight and shadow, standing on a snowy marble floor.

We were on the Pacific slope, and our plan was to cross the summit by the shortest way between timber-line there and timber-line on the Atlantic side. This meant ascending a thousand feet and descending an equal distance, traveling five miles amid bleak, rugged environment.

After gaining a thousand feet of altitude through the friendly forest, we climbed out and up above the trees on a steep slope at

OVERLEAF:
Enos Mills demonstrates snowshoe use
below Longs Peak near his inn.
These two photos present Mills as he saw himself
in the role of Colorado Snow Observer.
The snowshoe is held up so that it will show in the photos.
The photos were taken from two different angles.
These are not snapshots, but carefully composed images
designed to show what being
Colorado Snow Observer was all about.
It was not by accident that Mills included a dog
as a vital part of his role as investigator and
interpreter of Colorado wilderness.
DENVER PUBLIC LIBRARY, WESTERN HISTORY DEPARTMENT

timber-line. This place, the farthest up for trees, was a picturesque, desolate place. The dwarfed, gnarled, storm-shaped trees amid enormous snow-drifts told of endless, and at times deadly, struggles of the trees with the elements. Most of the trees were buried, but here and there a leaning or a storm-distorted one bent bravely above the snows.

Along the treeless, gradual ascent we started, realizing that the last steep icy climb would be dangerous and defiant. Most of the snow had slid from the steeper places, and much of the remainder had blown away. Over the unsheltered whole the wind was howling. For a time the sun shone dimly through the wind-driven snow-dust that rolled from the top of the range, but it disappeared early behind wild, wind-swept clouds.

At last we were safe on a ridge, and we started merrily off, hoping to cover speedily the three miles of comparatively level plateau.

How the wind did blow! Up more than eleven thousand feet above the sea, with not a tree to steady or break, it had a royal sweep. The wind appeared to be putting forth its wildest efforts to blow us off the ridge. There being a broad way, I kept well from the edges. The wind came with a dash and a heavy rush, first from one quarter, then from another. I was watchful and faced each rush firmly braced. Generally this preparedness saved me; but several times the wind seemed to expand or explode beneath me, and, with an upward toss, I was flung among the icy rocks and crusted snows. Finally I took to dropping and lying flat whenever a violent gust came ripping among the crags.

There was an arctic barrenness to this alpine ridge,—not a house within miles, no trail, and here no tree could live to soften the sternness of the landscape or to cheer the traveler. The way wound amid snowy piles, icy spaces, and wind-swept crags.

The wind slackened and snow began to fall just as we were leaving the smooth plateau for the broken part of the divide. The next mile of way was badly cut to pieces with deep gorges from both sides of the ridge. The inner ends of several of these broke through the center of the ridge and extended beyond the ends of the gorges from the opposite side. This made the course a series of sharp, short zigzags.

We went forward in the flying snow. I could scarcely see, but felt that I could keep the way on the broken ridge between the numerous rents and cañons. On snowy, icy ledges the wind took reckless liberties. I wanted to stop but dared not, for the cold was intense enough to freeze one in a few minutes.

Fearing that a snow-whirl might separate us, I fastened one end of my light, strong rope to Scotch's collar and the other end to my belt. This proved to be fortunate for both, for while we were crossing an icy, though moderate, slope, a gust of wind swept me off my feet and started us sliding. It was not steep, but was so slippery I could not stop, nor see where the slope ended, and I grabbed in vain at the few icy projections. Scotch also lost his footing and was sliding and rolling about, and the wind was hurrying us along, when I threw myself flat and dug at the ice with fingers and toes. In the midst of my unsuccessful efforts we were brought to a sudden stop by the rope between us catching over a small rock-point that was thrust up through the ice. Around this in every direction was smooth, sloping ice; this, with the high wind, made me wonder for a moment how we were to get safely off the slope. The belt axe proved the means, for with it I reached out as far as I could and chopped a hole in the ice, while with the other hand I clung to the rock-point. Then, returning the axe to my belt, I caught hold in the chopped place and pulled myself forward, repeating this until on safe footing.

In oncoming darkness and whirling snow I had safely rounded the ends of two gorges and was hurrying forward over a comparatively level stretch, with the wind at my back boosting me along. Scotch was running by my side and evidently was trusting me to guard against all dangers. This I tried to do. Suddenly, however, there came a fierce dash of wind and whirl of snow that hid everything. Instantly I flung myself flat, trying to stop quickly. Just as I did this I caught the strange, weird sound made by high wind as it sweeps across a cañon, and at once realized that we were close to a storm-hidden gorge. I stopped against a rock, while Scotch slid into the chasm and was hauled back with the rope.

The gorge had been encountered between two out-thrusting side gorges, and between these in the darkness I had a cold time feeling my way out. At last I came to a cairn of stones that I recognized. I had missed the way by only a few yards, but this miss had been nearly fatal.

Not daring to hurry in the darkness in order to get warm, I was becoming colder every moment. I still had a stiff climb between me and the summit, with timberline three rough miles beyond. To attempt to make it would probably result in freezing or tumbling into a gorge. At last I realized that I must stop and spend the night in a snow-drift. Quickly kicking and trampling a trench in a loose drift, I placed my elkskin sleeping-bag therein, thrust Scotch into the bag, and then squeezed into it myself.

I was almost congealed with cold. My first thought after warming up was to wonder why I had not earlier remembered the bag. Two in a bag would guarantee warmth, and with warmth, a snow-drift on the crest of the continent would not be a bad place in which to lodge for the night.

The sounds of wind and snow beating upon the bag grew fainter and fainter as we were drifted and piled over with the snow. At the same time our temperature rose, and before long it was necessary to open the flap of the bag slightly for ventilation.

At last the sounds of the storm could barely be heard. Was the storm quieting down, or was its roar muffled and lost in the deepening cover of snow? was the unimportant question occupying my thoughts when I fell asleep.

Scotch awakened me in trying to get out of the bag. It was morning. Out we crawled, and, standing with only my head above the drift, I found the air still and saw a snowy mountain world all serene in the morning sun. I hastily adjusted sleeping-bag and snowshoes, and we set off for the final climb to the summit.

The final hundred feet or so rose steep, jagged, and ice-covered before me. There was nothing to lay hold of; every point of vantage was plated with smooth ice. There appeared only one way to surmount this icy barrier and that was to chop toe- and hand-holes from the bottom to the top of this icy wall, which in places was close to vertical. Such a climb would not be especially difficult or dangerous for me, but could Scotch do it? He could hardly know how to place his feet in the holes or on the steps properly; nor could he realize that a slip or a misstep would mean a slide and a roll to death.

Leaving sleeping-bag and snowshoes with Scotch, I grasped my axe and chopped my way to the top and then went down and carried bag and snowshoes up. Returning for Scotch, I started him climbing just ahead of me, so that I could boost and encourage him. We had gained only a few feet when it became plain that sooner or later he would slip and bring disaster to both of us. We stopped and descended to the bottom for a new start.

Though the wind was again blowing a gale, I determined to carry him. His weight was forty pounds, and he would make a top-heavy load and give the wind a good chance to upset my balance and tip me off the wall.

But, as there appeared no other way, I threw him over my shoulder and started up.

Many times Scotch and I had been in ticklish places together, and more than once I had pulled him up rocky cliffs on which he could not find footing. Several times I had carried him over gulches on fallen logs that were too slippery for him. He was so trusting and so trained that he relaxed and never moved while in my arms or on my shoulder.

Arriving at the place least steep, I stopped to transfer Scotch from one shoulder to the other. The wind was at its worst; its direction frequently changed and it alternately calmed and then came on like an explosion. For several seconds it had been roaring down the slope; bracing myself to withstand its force from this direction, I was about to move

Scotch, when it suddenly shifted to one side and came with the force of a breaker. It threw me off my balance and tumbled me heavily against the icy slope.

Though my head struck solidly, Scotch came down beneath me and took most of the shock. Instantly we glanced off and began to slide swiftly. Fortunately I managed to get two fingers into one of the chopped holes and held fast. I clung to Scotch with one arm; we came to a stop, both saved. Scotch gave a yelp of pain when he fell beneath me, but he did not move. Had he made a jump or attempted to help himself, it is likely that both of us would have gone to the bottom of the slope.

Gripping Scotch with one hand and clinging to the icy hold with the other, I shuffled about until I got my feet into two holes in the icy wall. Standing in these and leaning against the ice, with the wind butting and dashing, I attempted the ticklish task of lifting Scotch again to my shoulder—and succeeded. A minute later we paused to breathe on the summit's icy ridge, between two oceans and amid seas of snowy peaks.

V

One cold winter day we were returning from a four days' trip on the Continental Divide, when, a little above timber-line, I stopped to take some photographs. To do this it was necessary for me to take off my sheep-skin mittens, which I placed in my coat pocket, but not securely, as it proved. From time to time, as I climbed to the summit of the Divide, I stopped to take photographs, but on the summit the cold pierced my silk gloves and I felt for my mittens, to find that one of them was lost. I stooped, put an arm around Scotch and told him that I had lost a mitten and that I wanted him to go down for it to save me the trouble. "It won't take you very long," I said, "but it will be a hard trip for me. Go and fetch it to me."

Instead of starting off quickly and willingly as he had invariably done before in obedience to my commands, he stood still. His eager, alert ears drooped. He did not make a move. I repeated the command in my most kindly tones. At this, instead of starting down the mountain for the mitten, he slunk slowly away toward home. Apparently he did not want to climb down the steep, icy slope of a mile to timber-line, more than a thousand feet below. I thought he had misunderstood me, so I called him back, patted him, and then, pointing down the slope, said,

"Go for the mitten, Scotch; I will wait for you here." He started, but went unwillingly. He had always served me so cheerfully that I could not understand his behavior, and it was not until later that I realized how cruelly he had misunderstood.

The summit of the Continental Divide where I stood when I sent Scotch back, was a very rough and lonely region. On every hand were broken, snowy peaks and rugged cañons. My cabin, eighteen miles away, was the nearest house, and the region was utterly wild.

I waited a reasonable time for Scotch to return, but he did not come back. Thinking he might have gone by without my seeing him, I walked some distance along the summit, first in one direction and then in the other, but, seeing neither him nor his tracks, I knew that he had not yet returned. As it was late in the afternoon and growing colder, I decided to go slowly on toward my cabin. I started along a route I felt sure he would follow and I reasoned that he would overtake me. Darkness came on and still no Scotch, but I kept on going forward. For the remainder of the way I told myself that he might have got by me in the darkness.

When, at midnight, I arrived at the cabin, I expected to be greeted by him. He was not there. I felt that something was wrong and feared that he had met with an accident. I slept two hours and rose, but he was still missing. I decided to tie on my snowshoes and go to meet him. The thermometer showed fourteen degrees below zero.

I started at three o'clock in the morning, feeling that I should meet him before going far. I kept on and on and when at noon I arrived at the place on the summit from which I had sent him back, Scotch was not there to cheer the wintry, silent scene.

Slowly I made my way down the slope and at two in the afternoon, twenty-four hours after I had sent Scotch down the mountain, I paused on a crag and looked below. There, in a world of white, Scotch lay by the mitten in the snow. He had misunderstood me and had gone back to guard the mitten instead of to get it.

He could hardly contain himself for joy when we met. He leaped into the air, barked, rolled over, licked my hand, whined, seized the mitten in his mouth, raced round and round me, and did everything that an alert, affectionate, faithful dog could to show that he appreciated my appreciation of his supremely faithful services.

After waiting for him to eat a luncheon we started for home, where we arrived at one o'clock in the morning. Had I not gone back for Scotch, I suppose he would have died beside the mitten. Without food or companionship, in a region cold, cheerless, and oppressive, he was watching the mitten because he had understood that I had told him to watch it. In the annals of the dog I do not know of any more touching instance of loyalty.

VI

Through the seasons and through the years Scotch and I wandered in the wilds and enjoyed nature together. Though we were often wet, hungry, or cold, he never ceased to be cheerful. Through the scenes and the silences we went side by side; side by side in the lonely night we gazed into the camp-fire, and in feeling lived strangely through "yesterday's seven thousand years" together.

He was only a puppy the first time that he went with me to enjoy the woods. During this trip we came upon an unextinguished camp-fire that was spreading and about to become a forest fire. Upon this fire I fell with utmost speed so as to extinguish it before it should enlarge beyond control. My wild stampings, beatings, and hurling of fire-brands made a deep impression on puppy Scotch. For a time he stood still and watched me, and then he jumped in and tried to help. He bit and clawed at the flames, burned himself, and with deep growlings desperately shook smoking sticks.

The day following this incident, as we strolled through the woods, he came upon another smouldering camp-fire and at once called my attention to it with lively barking. I patted him and tried to make him understand that I appreciated what he had done, and then extinguished the fire. Through the years, in our wood wanderings, he was alert for fire and prompt to warn me of a discovery. His nose and eye detected many fires that even my trained and watchful senses had missed.

One autumn, while watching a forest fire, we became enveloped in smoke and narrowly escaped with our lives. The fire had started in the bottom and was burning upward in the end of a long, wide mountain valley, and giving off volumes of smoke. In trying to obtain a clearer view, and also to avoid the smoke, we descended into a ravine close behind the fire. Shortly after our arrival a strong wind drove the wings of the fire outward to right and left, then backward down both sides of the valley, filling the ravine with smoke.

This movement of the fire would in a short time have encircled us with flames. I made a dash to avoid this peril, and in running along a rock ledge in the smoke, stumbled into a rocky place and one of my shoes stuck fast. This threw me heavily and badly sprained my left leg. Amid thick smoke, falling ashes, and approaching flames, this situation was a serious one. Scotch showed the deepest concern by staying close by me and finally by giving a number of strange barks such as I had never before heard. After freeing myself I was unable to walk, and in hopping and creeping along my camera became so annoying that I gave it to Scotch; but in the brush the straps became so often entangled that throwing it away proved a relief to us both.

Mills shows his regard for his co-host of Longs Peak Inn
on the porch of the main building.

Meanwhile we were making slow progress through the unburned woods and the fire was roaring close. Seeing no hope of getting out of the way, we finally took refuge to the leeward side of a rocky crag where the flames could not reach us. But could we avoid being smothered? Already we were dangerously near that and the fire had yet to surge around us. To send Scotch for water offered a possible means of escape. Slapping my coat upon the rocks two or three times I commanded, "Water, Scotch, water!" He understood, and with an eager bark seized the coat and vanished in the smoke. He would be compelled to pass through a line of flame in order to reach the water in the ravine, but this he would do or die.

After waiting a reasonable time I began to call, "Scotch! Scotch!" as loudly as my parched throat and gasping permitted. Presently he leaped upon me, fearfully burned but with the saturated coat in his teeth. Most of his shaggy coat was seared off, one eye was closed, and there was a cruel burn on his left side. Hurriedly I bound a coat-sleeve around his head to protect his eyes and nose, then squeezed enough water from the coat to wet my throat. Hugging Scotch closely, I spread the wet coat over us both and covered my face with a wet hand-kerchief. With stifling smoke and fiery heat the flames surged around, but at last swept over and left us both alive. Without the help from Scotch I must have perished.

It was this useful fire-fighting habit that caused the death of my faithful Scotch. One morning the men started off to do some road work. Scotch saw them go and apparently wanted to go with them. I had just returned from a long absence and had to stay in the cabin and write letters. About half an hour after the men had gone, Scotch gave a scratching knock at the door. Plainly he wanted to follow the men and had come for my consent to go without me. I patted him and urged him to go. He left he cabin, never again to return.

Scotch arrived at the road work just as the men had lighted and run away from a blast. He saw the smoking fuse and sprang to extinguish it, as the blast exploded. He was instantly killed.

THE END

THE LEGACY OF SCOTCH

by Kent Dannen

The power of civilization that killed Scotch was invincible, Mills knew. He maintained, however, that within civilization was the wisdom to preserve wild land to invigorate and inspire the human spirit. "In these wild parks," he wrote in his book *Your National Parks*, "we may rebuild the past . . . ," in order "to have and to hold high ideals" *(Bird Memories of the Rockies)*. Rocky Mountain National Park, one of the brightest and most valuable jewels among the national parks, was Mills' legacy to the world.

Scotch significantly enlarged this legacy by deepening Mills' wilderness understanding and appreciation during his important wilderness experiences from 1902 to 1910. For Mills, the point of preserving wild land was to enable succeeding generations of people to imitate Mills' experiences. They thereby could stay in contact with the rule of nature that guided humanity and "triumphantly leads us on" *(Enos Mills of the Rockies)*. Dogs that help people understand and appreciate wild nature are the successors of Scotch and are his legacy to the world.

This canine influence has been important in developing the ideas of other important leaders of American conservation, including John Muir, Aldo Leopold, and Bob Marshall. As they did for Mills, Muir, Leopold, and Marshall, dogs can boost appreciation of wilderness values for today's hikers in at least six ways: (1) Dogs enhance the positive power of play (see Foreword). (2) Dogs provide the best possible link between human and nonhuman perceptions of the world. (3) Dogs share superior senses of smell and hearing with human companions. (4) Dogs serve as pack animals, thereby making room in human packs for nature interpretation aids such as cameras, binoculars, magnifying lenses, and guidebooks. (5) Dogs connect modern hikers and past hikers, giving us a better sense of history and place. (6) Dogs increase human sense of wilderness solitude.

As John Muir preceded Enos Mills, Stickeen preceded Scotch. Muir in 1880 explored Taylor Glacier in Alaska's Glacier Bay National Park with a mixed-breed dog named Stickeen. Through Stickeen, Muir gained his greatest insight about how all living things are connected to each other. Although humans helped develop dogs and dogs perhaps brought about certain traits that we now identify as human, dogs still have a couple of paws in the world of wild canines. Because people can identify with dogs, we also can gain wild predators' perceptions of the world and eventually gain the viewpoint of all animals.

On what Muir described as "the most memorable of all my wild days," storm and glacial crevasses came very close to killing both explorers. In this time of mutual stress, Stickeen revealed a dog's unique ability to bestow to humans an understanding of wild animals from which we are otherwise completely cut off.

Of their survival Muir wrote, "I have known many dogs, and many a story I could tell of their wisdom and devotion; but to none do I owe so much as to Stickeen. At first the least promising and least known of my dog friends, he suddenly became the best known of them all. Our storm-battle for life brought him to light, and through him as through a window I have ever since been looking with deeper sympathy into all my fellow mortals." (*Stickeen: The Story of a Dog*) It was this sympathy for the nonhuman universe that motivated John Muir to become the most effective and inspirational person within the conservation movement. Among those he inspired was Enos Mills.

John Muir was the prime prophet of wilderness preservation, and Aldo Leopold a generation later became wilderness preservation's most important philosopher. His main influence has been through one small collection of finely honed essays, *A Sand County Almanac.* I asked Leopold's daughter, Nina Leopold Bradley, how it was that her father generated so many significant insights from the same experiences that many other people enjoy. She was there as a teenager when her father was living the events that inspired his famous *Almanac*, and she replied, "He had a modesty that allowed him to learn from his dogs."

Leopold himself cast his German Shorthaired Pointer in the role of a professor teaching Leopold to observe closely what happened around him in nature: "My dog . . . persists in tutoring me, with the calm patience of professor of logic, in the art of drawing deductions from an educated nose. I delight in seeing him deduce a conclusion, in the form of a point, from data that are obvious to him, but speculative to my unaided eye. Perhaps he hopes his dull pupil will one day learn to smell."

At another time, Leopold's dog was a professor of literature, translating "for me the olfactory poems that who-knows-what silent creatures have written in the summer light."

Clearly Leopold learned very well to translate what his own and his dogs' senses revealed in nature. He logically deduced the value of wilderness and the necessity of a land ethic and expressed them not only logically but beautifully. *A Sand County Almanac* is the philosophical basis of the conservation movement and also a classic masterpiece of American literature.

Bob Marshall led governmental involvement in Leopold's land ethic. Independently wealthy, Marshall advanced the cause of wilderness preservation as a bureaucrat, working himself literally to death for the sake of his goals. He undertook backpacking trips of awesome effort to explore potential wilderness areas and popularized their values through accounts of his explorations.

Marshall carried huge loads on these trips, placing stress on his heart that many blamed for his death at a young age. Many baby-boomers suffering from skeletal and connective-tissue ailments due to carrying heavy packs during the hiking boom of the 1960s and 1970s can empathize with his problems.

They also can benefit from the partial solution Marshall used while exploring in Alaska — using pack dogs to help lessen the load. The same help is available to parents who need to carry many extra things to introduce children to the wilderness. These children will be the future users and defenders of wilderness. When dogs are toting extra clothing, food, water, and first-aid supplies, more room opens in human packs for cameras, magnifying lenses, and guidebooks.

While photographing beargrass near the edge of Bob Marshall Wilderness, Donna Dannen gets advice from son Pat and help in hauling gear from Ch. Snowflower Spun Sugar, CD, WS.

PHOTO BY KENT AND DONNA DANNEN

From the standpoint of Marshall's bureaucratic successors who manage wilderness areas today, dogs can be ideal pack animals. They cause no trail erosion, do not graze extensively on trailside vegetation, and are easy to transport to trailheads, requiring no additional room for parked vehicles.

Using dogs to supplement weak human senses as Leopold did or using them as pack animals as Marshall did provides modern hikers with our only direct link with previous generations of wilderness users. Archeology indicates that dogs have been part of American wilderness for 11,000 years, longer than some of the wild animals and plants. Though leather does not survive like a stone projectile point, we can assume that the leash and dog pack are among the oldest human inventions in North America. Documents dating from the Lewis and Clark Expedition through modern times indicate the role that dogs played more recently in helping humans cope with wilderness.

Marshall effectively bolstered the case for preserving wilderness when he wrote, "It is the last stand for that glorious adventure into the physically unknown that was commonplace in the lives of our ancestors." In another reference to wilderness adventure, Marshall wrote of preferring to "mush dogs with adventure than to have the luxury and restrictions of the modern world."

Yet, modern wilderness users unavoidably approach the wilds with attitudes and expectations completely different from humans even a few generations ago. They viewed the wilds as human habitat from which to wrench a living rather than as a recreational resource. Earning a living in the wilds was hard, and death for a variety of reasons was not surprising. Today's travelers in the wilds get their food from supermarkets, wear high-tech garb for protection, and in the case of misadventure, expect ranger rescue.

Our technology and our different attitudes separate us unavoidably from adventurers who preceded us in the wilds. To the stoneage ghost watching modern hikers from behind a tree, we are no less strange than if we had come down from the stars. The only thing about us that a ghost can recognize is our relationship to our dogs.

Links to the past are important to experiencing wilderness because history gives us a sense of place, of where we stand today. Without a sense of place, most other wilderness values become greatly diminished.

History, in fact, is implied in all wilderness values. Our society preserves wilderness in order that individuals may rediscover the values that historic prophets and philosophers like Muir, Mills, Leopold, and Marshall have found there. If we no longer can duplicate the experiences of the prophets, the point of wilderness preservation is lost.

Muir, Mills, and Leopold made great discoveries about wilderness values while alone in the wilds with only their dogs' companionship. This experience of solitude within companionship remains available to many people today who perhaps need it more than the prophets did.

Humans evolved from animals that lived in packs. Many humans suffer from genetic discomfort with solitude that causes ambivalence about the value of being alone in the wilds. This discomfort may cause some hikers to exaggerate fears of potential dangers from other humans or from wildlife in

Patrick Dannen enjoys hiking with his champion Samoyed pack dog, Parka, above the Colorado River in Utah's Dead Horse Point State Park.
PHOTO BY KENT AND DONNA DANNEN

the wilderness. Fears detract from other wilderness values.

Canine companionship allows some hikers to have the benefits of solitude from other people without the natural discomfort of solitude. Also derived from animals that lived in packs, dogs can provide

*Donna Dannen rests with her Samoyed pack dogs,
Karibou and Chinook, while hiking in the
Indian Peaks Wilderness, Colorado.*
PHOTO BY KENT AND DONNA DANNEN

the pack's sense of safety and well-being without detracting from the relief that some wilderness users seek from pressures of human contact.

Moreover, dogs can increase the sense of solitude that sometimes is hard to find in wilderness areas with easy access from urban areas. Most of the many visitors to these wilderness areas come from an urban environment where they have learned with justification to be wary of strangers. The actual value of such wariness usually is slight in the wilds, but good urban habits are hard to leave behind at the trailhead. More by their companionship than by their real defensive value, dogs help to reduce exaggerated fears stimulated by other wilderness visitors who are present but probably not dangerous.

With the fear stimulated by fellow wilderness users reduced by canine companionship, a sense of solitude from those other users is much easier to maintain. When dogs eliminate concern over other people from a person's mind, those other people may disappear from vision and consciousness. In this case, the truth is "out of mind, out of sight," and a sense of solitude naturally increases.

*Patrick Dannen enjoys hiking with his Samoyed,
Ch. Sylvan Parka of Tundra Winds, WSXM.*
PHOTO BY KENT AND DONNA DANNEN

These six ways in which dogs can increase wilderness values for their human companions have benefitted society greatly through canine influence on great leaders like Mills, Muir, Leopold, and Marshall. Perhaps even more value, however, has come from dogs' influence on thousands of anonymous hikers. Though facts about how many people hike with dogs are hard to find, USDA Forest Service records indicate that between 20,000 and 25,000 people a year enjoy canine companionship in the Indian Peaks Wilderness, land that Mills and others proposed for inclusion in Rocky Mountain National Park.

Only a tiny percentage of wilderness visitors will use their canine wilderness companions as effectively as Mills used Scotch. Even little bits of good, however, when multiplied by thousands, become very significant for society very quickly.

Donna Dannen with Spinner and Chinook on leashes just outside Rocky Mountain National Park.

PHOTO BY KENT AND DONNA DANNEN

THE MODERNIZATION OF SCOTCH

by Kent Dannen

It should be no surprise that anything of such great value as canine companionship in the wilds is not free. You have to work and sweat to gain the benefits of climbing a mountain (although somewhat less if you are pulled up by a dog). Analogous costs and responsibilities are associated with hiking with dogs. In both cases, the value received is many times the cost.

Standing on the shoulders of our predecessors in the wilds, we can learn from their experiences and pay a somewhat smaller cost for our enjoyment of wilderness. Modern boots work better than Mills' hob-nailed boots. Synthetic jackets are better than his elk-skin coat. It still is hard to beat Mills' raisins, but at least lighter, processed foods can add variety to wilderness eating. Preparing such foods on light-weight backpacking stoves beats wood fires in many different ways.

As I thumb again through *The Story of Scotch,* I note various ways in which nearly a century of experience with dogs has improved our techniques of using and loving modern representatives of Scotch.

(1) In the first chapter, Mills mentions that Scotch slept in an old tub outside Mills' cabin throughout the year. Though Mills evidently viewed this as a compliment to his dog's hardiness, this would not be adequate shelter by modern standards. When pet dogs spend a good deal of time inside with their owners, the bond of communication and companionship increases. Hikers who are less perceptive than the remarkable Mills almost surely need to strengthen this bond as much as possible.

(2) Mills refers to Scotch drinking from streams and ponds. Now, as then, this practice, whether by humans or dogs, certainly leads to illness. For instance, both human doctors and veterinarians frequently need to treat their patients for giardia, caused by a parasite found in nearly all untreated water. The ailment's most evident symptoms are diarrhea, flatulence, and cramps. Dogs have no special protection from the effects of drinking dirty water and no special

Patrick Dannen pauses from hiking in the Indian Peaks Wilderness; water supplied by his Samoyed pack dogs, Spinner and Glacier.

PHOTO BY KENT AND DONNA DANNEN

sense for distinguishing good water from bad. Make every effort to prevent them from drinking any water considered unfit for human consumption. This means keeping them on a leash when you hike and having them carry their own water in dog packs.

(3) Dogs should not be fed outside, where uneaten food in Scotch's Colorado territory is virtually certain to draw wildlife. Feeding wild animals should be done only with much care and thought, not as a coincidental side effect of feeding a dog. Wild animals may contaminate dog food left outside, perhaps spreading disease to dogs and even humans. Feeding a dog outside probably means that an owner does not know how much a dog is eating, the reason why obesity probably is an even greater problem among dogs than among humans. The list of wild animals drawn to dog food set outside includes many species that change from very valuable assets to pests when they associate too closely with humans. This effect ranges from tiny deer mice to raccoons, deer, bears, and mountain lions.

(4) Mills boasted that Scotch was very moderate in his barking, only alerting Mills to events that

needed his attention. Barking is an important means of canine communication and within reason one of a dog's most useful traits. An Estes Park neighbor once approached me about my dogs' barking. He mildly complained that I did not permit my dogs to bark enough. My neighbor considered my dogs alerting him to what was going on around our houses as a service. Police departments almost always encourage home owners to buy a dog that barks as a better defense against intruders than a gun.

As it happened, I did not permit my dogs to increase their barking because they were my most prized possessions. I considered it poor policy to flaunt my most prized possessions before the world and therefore kept my dogs semi-inconspicuous. So my neighbor acquired his own dog that barked.

(5) One of the most amazing accounts in *The Story of Scotch* tells of his war with coyotes, his plotting against the wild canines, and his recruiting another dog as an ally in the war (pages 16–20). Today, it is very unlikely that dog owners will be pleased with the outcomes of such conflicts. Wounds from coyotes make up a large part of the

veterinary practice in Estes Park, and fatalities among pets are common.

Letting a dog roam unfenced today is irresponsible when done in ignorance and immoral when done after having been warned. Not only is there danger from wildlife (primarily coyotes, but also mountain lions, badgers, and even mild-mannered deer or elk) but also from motor vehicles. Killed before the road was even finished, Scotch ranks not only among Estes Park's most famous dogs, but also qualifies as its first canine road fatality. Accidental poisoning also is a significant threat. So-called safe poisons aimed at rodents or coyotes present a danger to pets that Scotch probably did not face.

Of course, dogs themselves are predators and will harass wildlife if allowed to roam unfenced. Most dogs are comparatively poor predators. If they should catch and consume the occasional bunny or rodent, however, the dogs almost always will contract some sort of noxious worm from their prey.

Dogs are highly unlikely to kill large animals like deer or elk. However, harassing these grazers during winter could put the deer or elk at significant disadvantage in surviving the rigors of the season. In spring, a dog could kill a fawn or elk calf.

Because people wiped out the wolves and grizzly bears that entertained Mills and taught him valuable lessons about the wilds, Scotch's old territory is definitely predator poor. Because deer and elk populations face far less than natural predation, dogs will not exert any negative influence on total deer and elk numbers even though dogs might indirectly cause the death of an individual animal. Nonetheless, to have dogs harassing the big grazers amounts to unnecessary human interference with deer and elk, which you should avoid. Keep the dogs fenced and leashed.

(6) My favorite of the Scotch stories tells of the dog being entrusted to guide a novice climber up Longs Peak in today's Rocky Mountain National Park (pages 20–25). At present, however, Rocky Mountain National Park regulations ban all dogs from trails, even if the dogs are leashed.

On page 40, Mills refers to the Grand River, later renamed the Colorado River. Therefore, this adventure of Mills and Scotch likely occurred in the vicinity of Bighorn Flats and Flattop Mountain.

On page 61, Mills writes that he stood on the Continental Divide eighteen miles from his cabin. I guess that Scotch therefore guarded Mills' glove on the west side of Flattop Mountain. However, this example of faithfulness might have occurred on the west side of Boulder–Grand Pass. In either case, Mills did some astounding hiking, proving the supreme value he placed on Scotch.

(7) Mills wrote of Scotch cheering a stern landscape. This seems an odd statement from a man who clearly loved the mountain landscape deeply. Humans who spend as much time as Mills did in the wilderness often come to realize that some thrilling and beautiful areas of the mountains are naturally hostile to human life. Especially above tree line, the wind is a cruel tyrant, determined to kill every living thing that fails to prostrate itself less than six inches above the ground.

On the heights, climbers stare across vast, windswept distances devoid of trees and vaulted by endless sky. To describe this landscape as merely stern seems an understatement close to bravado. Such a scene, though romantic and dramatic, can reduce human self-esteem to the height of tundra flowers. The

*Patrick Dannen signs register atop Meadow Mountain, Indian
Peaks Wilderness, Colorado, accompanied by his Samoyed
pack dogs Parka and Bruin.*
PHOTO BY KENT AND DONNA DANNEN

sense of human insignificance probably is beneficial
in moderate doses, but it also can be depressing and
as deadly as the wind which can pick up a climber
and pin him or her to a rock like a butterfly. That Mills
so rarely commented on this character of the heights is

a measure of his strong personality and spirit.

It may be also a measure of the influence of Scotch, who joined up with Mills at the same time that his Colorado Snow Observer job thrust Mills onto the heights often in fierce winter. I have experienced my own dogs' capacity to lift my spirit above the tundra's disturbing intimidation to a higher level of appreciation for mountain-top grandeur. My Samoyed pack dogs are similar enough to Border Collies to make me understand how Scotch could have elevated Mills' spirit and appreciation of the heights and cheered a stern landscape indeed.

(8) One significant difference between my Samoyeds and Border Collies like Scotch stems from their ancestral purposes. Samoyeds were bred originally by nomadic tribes in Siberia to pull sleds, carry packs, and drive herds of reindeer over great distances. Border Collies were bred in the also harsh Scottish Highlands to prevent sheep from scattering over great distances. Hence, Mills could rely on Scotch to stay near at hand and perform as instructed far more than I can trust my dogs, who mainly want to see the far side of the ridge as soon as possible.

*Donna Dannen and Spinner are happy to see that dogs on
leash are allowed to enjoy the trails at
Salinas National Monument, New Mexico.*

PHOTO BY KENT AND DONNA DANNEN

Mills got away with leaving Scotch unleashed fairly often, while I never allow my dogs such freedom. There are advantages to leashing my dogs that Mills likely never considered. For instance, my sled dogs often drag me up trails, making the ascent easier and faster than you would believe unless you had experienced it. Once on top, descent in the same fashion at even greater speed can be problematic. (Switching to a more restrictive collar helps considerably.)

Even taking differences among breeds of dogs and between individual dogs into account, leashing all dogs while hiking today is the best policy. The managers of many of the finest hiking areas where dogs still are permitted often require leashes. Failing to abide by the leash regulation seriously endangers opportunities for all future hikers to benefit from improved use of the wilderness through canine companionship.

Regulations aside, other significant advantages argue in favor of keeping dogs leashed. Leashes protect dogs with less wilderness experience than Scotch had from natural hazards, such as porcupines, predators, and precipices. Mills tells of tying Scotch to his body with a rope, the equivalent of a

*Donna Dannen and Tundra pause from ski touring
to remove a glove from the pack.*
PHOTO BY KENT AND DONNA DANNEN

leash, in order to keep the dog from plunging down steep, snow-covered slopes.

A similar practice while skijoring (being pulled on skis by a dog) enabled me to easily rescue my dog, Chinook, from a hole in the snow that had collapsed from her weight above a stream. She could not, however, climb out. Though not in the water, she surely would have been as she became weary and probably would have drowned in a natural trap. Because rescue was so easy, her predicament was more amusing than frightening (though her screaming did not seem to reveal an appreciation of the humor). Had she been running free without the skijoring line, however, the result could have been death for Chinook and heartbreak for me.

One advantage of my dogs' Arctic background is their tendency to avoid getting wet. They diligently walk around mud puddles in the trail when they can, though they love cooling off in snow. Scotch seems not to have cared much for getting wet (aside from a morning bath), a trait that Mills probably appreciated as much in his dog as I do in mine. Owners of popular sporting breeds, such as Golden Retrievers or Labrador Retrievers, know well their dogs' determination to swim whenever possible. Using leashes to keep dogs out of the water avoids many inconveniences for hikers.

Only leashes can prevent even my dogs and Scotch-like Border Collies from lapping water from

Tundra cools off in a snowbank after carrying her pack up the steep trail to Caribou Pass, Indian Peaks Wilderness.
PHOTO BY KENT AND DONNA DANNEN

ponds and streams. Of course, Mills often drank from such water sources himself. Doubtless both Mills and Scotch suffered illness from time to time as a result of this practice. Dogs that hike unleashed definitely will get giardia and/or some other water-carried illness sooner or later—probably sooner.

Donna Dannen hiking with pack dog, Ch. Wind River
Talkeetna Karibou, CD, WSXM, at Caribou Pass, for which
he was named, in the Indian Peaks Wilderness.
PHOTO BY KENT AND DONNA DANNEN

Moreover, leashed dogs are far more likely to share their superior senses of smell and hearing with their humans. When accompanied by a leashed dog, hikers are virtually certain to see more wildlife than they would notice without that dog. If accompanied by an unleashed dog, they may see somewhat less wildlife, unless the dog is a very well-trained member of one of the sporting breeds, field-trial champion quality. Accustomed to far deadlier predators than dogs, the wild animals do not care much whether or not the dogs are leashed, but the critters easily will avoid unleashed dogs in ways that are likely to make the wild animals invisible to hikers.

Moreover, an unleashed dog may encounter another human hiker who happens to be tragically afraid of dogs. This condition is analogous to fear of heights, fear of confined spaces, or fear of crowds. It is no more appropriate to inflict an unleashed dog on a person already much afflicted by fear than it would be to jerk away a seeing-eye dog from a blind person.

A person who fears dogs automatically loses huge benefits of wilderness experience. It seems unfair for hikers who enjoy superior benefits through canine companionship to let dogs run loose and thereby further decrease the already inferior benefits of wilderness experienced by this person.

‿

Patrick Dannen rests from hiking with his Samoyed pack dog,
Ch. Tundra Winds' Arctic Gentian, WSX, at Long Lake
in the Indian Peaks Wilderness.

PACKING WITH SCOTCH

by Kent Dannen

Enos Mills did not use Scotch as a pack dog, but modern hikers can benefit much from this practice. Canine hikers also benefit from carrying packs because dogs need handicaps to benefit physically from the same amounts of exercise that benefit their human owners.

Dog packs have the same wide price range as human packs. Most outdoor-equipment stores report good sales of dog packs, yet my dogs' packs generate many surprised comments from other hikers (and offers to buy my dogs on the spot). Evidently, many dog packs gather dust in closets instead of on the trail.

Here are some tips to help get dog packs out of closets and onto dogs:

For a good fit, pack bags should hang from the top of the dog's back, not bulging out from a broad-backed dog or dragging too low. A breast band will help focus the weight over the shoulders rather than at midback. Padding helps thinly coated dogs. Double bottoms on the packs protect your possessions, which you should wrap in plastic bags.

Teach the dog not to bump the pack into things by having the dog wear the pack around the house (filled with light items). Later, the dog learns that his pack is a signal of good times ahead. Gradually condition dogs to carry 25 percent of their body weight as the hike begins. Consumption of water and food will reduce that weight.

Pack first-aid items for the dog as well as for yourself, including tweezers or needle-nosed pliers. (Porcupine quills lying on the ground have punctured the pads and noses of my leashed dogs.) Dog boots (available from sporting-goods stores or dog-supply catalogs) might be handy to protect pads from laceration or to allow a dog to walk out on an injured foot. Buffered aspirin and over-the-counter diarrhea remedies can help dogs, too. Be sure to ask your veterinarian about brands and dosages for your dog's size. Some remedies that benefit humans can harm dogs. Be sure that your dog is up on all of his shots; rabies does occur among wild animals.

Pack an extra leash in case yours breaks or in case you encounter someone else's loose dog. Also

"Thanks for bringing me." Pack dogs Winter and Parka both
are AKC champions and holders of the Samoyed Club of
America's top working title, Master Working Samoyed
(WSXM).

PHOTO BY KENT AND DONNA DANNEN

take along a dog comb or brush to remove seeds
and dirt. Some seeds can work their way into a dog's
skin and eventually cause painful, expensive injury.
Furthermore, if we meet on the trail, I want your dog
to look good for photos. From the predominance of

The Dannens backpacking with Samoyed pack dog,
Ch. Wind River Talkeetna Karibou, CD, WSXM.

PHOTO BY KENT AND DONNA DANNEN

Samoyed photos in this book, you can see that I need to photogaph other hikers' dogs.

Include a trowel in a plastic bag, not only to bury your own excrement, but also to remove dog feces from trails and away from water.

Have dogs carry their normal food. Sharing your food may cause digestive upset.

Your dogs should wear tags with your name and telephone number. Broken leashes or other unlikely accidents may separate human and canine hikers.

Do not let dogs approach other hikers unless the other hikers initiate the contact. Prevent dogs from barking continuously. If you meet parties with horses, mules, or llamas, move your dogs far enough off the trail to avoid disturbing the other animals.

Though many of these tips may seem negative, they really are not terribly burdensome. Often they are very important. They eventually will make hiking with your dog easier and will increase the canine fun that Enos Mills discovered to be a vital part of understanding and enjoying the wilderness.